Making Chests &
BOXES

GREG CHEETHAM

MINI · WORKBOOK · SERIES

MEREHURST

CONTENTS

Painted toy box (top), window seat (far left) and
traditional chest with curved lid (left).

Planning your projects

Wooden boxes and chests are functional and stylish pieces of furniture and there will be a suitable project in this book whether you are an experienced woodworker or weekend dabbler.

WORK AREA AND EQUIPMENT

You don't need a shed or workshop to make these wooden boxes and chests as long as you have a suitable, well-ventilated and well-lit area to work in. You will, however, need a workbench. There is a range of these available but a simple and cost-effective alternative is to get a pair of saw horses and lay a sturdy piece of chipboard across them. This makes a versatile workbench that will suit all of the projects in this book.

Most of the projects can be made using basic hand tools but if you are going to invest in some equipment, a circular saw, an electric drill, a jigsaw and a small portable router are the most commonly used power tools in home woodworking. Sometimes, the cost of a power tool is no more than the cost of the three or four hand tools—and power tools do save time and can give a more accurate result.

SAFETY PRECAUTIONS

When using any type of electric power tool, wear the correct safety equipment for the task. You will need safety goggles that enclose the eyes completely, a dust mask, hearing protection, and a cap or hairnet for any long hair (simply tying it back is not enough). It is also very important never to wear loose clothing when working with revolving machinery. Accidents happen very easily when tools with moving parts are used.

SELECTING TIMBER

A range of materials has been used to construct these boxes and chests, from solid wood to medium density fibreboard (MDF). For the projects that require solid wood, the selection of timber is important to the appearance of the finished job. Use good quality timber with few knots or other visible defects, and use plain sawn boards where possible as they are less likely to split. Choose a wood that is easy to work with. Check that the boards are straight by sighting down one long edge, and also check that they are not twisted along the length and are flat across their width.

Most large DIY stores will sell a limited selection of planed softwood timber in a range of sizes (often wrapped), and sometimes the planed size will be quoted rather than the nominal size (see box). The store may be able to cut timber to length.

A timber merchants is an alternative source and will have a

TIMBER CONDITIONS

Timber is sold in three conditions:
- sawn or rough sawn: sawn exactly to a specific (nominal) size
- planed-all-round (PAR): smoothed on all sides (by the timber supplier) to a size slightly smaller than nominal
- moulded: shaped to a specific profile for architraves, window sills, skirting boards and so on

Planed timber is mostly sold using the same nominal dimensions as sawn timber, for example 100 x 50 mm, but the surfaces have all been machined to a flat, even width and thickness so the '100 x 50 mm' timber is actually 95 x 45 mm. The chart shows the actual common sizes for softwood timber; these may vary with supplier—and hardwoods may be closer to nominal.

Where you need to join planks edge-to-edge, consider using laminated boards already joined.

Sawn (nominal) size (mm)	Size after dressing (mm)
16	12
19	15
22	18
25	21
38	34
50	45
75	70
100	95
125	120
150	145

larger choice of woods, including hardwoods. They will only deal in nominal sizes but they do have the necessary machinery to cut timber down in width and thickness, as well as cutting it roughly to length. You also have the chance to examine each piece of timber before you buy it: check that it is straight and has no defects such as knots or splits.

BEFORE YOU START

When you have chosen a project, read the instructions to gain an idea of what is involved. If you have not done much woodworking, practise the techniques, and particularly how to make the relevant joints, on scrap material before you start. Also use scrap material for a trial run before using pieces of equipment such as a circular saw or router (to check the blade or cutter setting).

Quality timber enhances beautiful woodwork such as dovetail joints.

Contrasting hardwoods, finished with clear lacquer, have been used to make this delightful box. Here, hard maple has been used for the main body, African paduak for the frames and beading, and bird's eye maple for the top panel.

Miniature treasure box

The construction of this beautiful treasure box is based on neat mitre joints and rebates. Contrasting timber is used for the frames and beading, and a feature panel on the lid completes the elegant and simple design.

TOOLS

- Tape measure
- Jack, block and smoothing planes
- Marking gauge
- Combination square and pencil
- Utility or marking knife
- Panel saw or circular saw
- Tenon saw
- Chisel: 25 mm bevelled-edge
- Rebate plane or router with a 12 mm straight cutting bit
- Electric drill
- Drill bits: 2 mm, 4 mm, countersink
- Mitre box or mitre saw (optional)
- Frame cramp
- Three quick-release cramps: 300 mm
- Cork sanding block or electric sander
- Screwdriver (cross-head or slotted)
- Fine nail punch and cabinet scraper

PREPARATION

1 If you are unable to buy 175 x 19 mm timber, use 100 x 19 mm and cut two pieces 280 mm long for the base. Place adhesive on one long edge of each and cramp together. Make sure the face sides are flush. Wipe off excess adhesive with a wet rag. Put the panel aside to dry.

2 For the sides and ends, straighten one long edge of a 0.9 m length of 100 x 19 mm timber with a jack plane and select a face side. Mark the width to 90 mm using a marking gauge and plane the timber to size.

3 Measure and mark the length of the sides and ends, making allowance for the saw cuts and final trimming. Square the lines with a combination square and pencil. Trace over the lines with a utility knife to cut the cross-grain fibres. Cramp the board to a bench and cut the parts slightly over length on the waste side of the lines with a panel or circular saw.

4 Place the end pieces face sides together in a vice and plane one end square and back to the knife lines. Turn the pieces over and plane the other end back to the lines. Use a sharp, finely-set block plane and work from each edge of the piece towards the centre so that you don't chip out the end grain.

5 Place the sides outside face down and draw lines the thickness of the ends (15 mm) from the knife lines for the rebates to hold the ends.

MATERIALS★

Part	Material	Finished length	No.
Sides	100 x 19 mm timber PAR	280 mm	2
Ends	100 x 19 mm timber PAR	152 mm	2
Base	175 x 19 mm timber PAR	266 mm	1
Top frame (sides)	75 x 25 mm timber PAR	300 mm	2
Top frame (ends)	75 x 25 mm timber PAR	200 mm	2
Top panel	100 x 25 mm timber PAR	188 mm	1
Beading (sides)	19 x 12 mm moulding	200 mm	2
Beading (ends)	19 x 12 mm moulding	100 mm	2
Lid rails (sides)	19 x 12 mm moulding	246 mm	2
Lid rails (ends)	19 x 12 mm moulding	132 mm	2
Bottom frame (sides)	50 x 19 mm timber PAR	320 mm	2
Bottom frame (ends)	50 x 19 mm timber PAR	200 mm	2

OTHER: PVA adhesive; six 25 mm (1 in) x No.6 gauge countersunk steel wood screws (cross-head or slotted); six 20 mm (3/4 in) x No.6 gauge countersunk steel wood screws (cross-head or slotted); ten 15 mm panel pins; clear lacquer; wood filler (to match timber colour); very fine steel wool; abrasive paper: sheet of 180 grade, sheet of 240 grade and one sheet of very fine wet-and-dry

★ Timber sizes are nominal (see page 5). This project requires: 0.9 m of 100 x 19 mm timber, 0.3 m of 175 x 19 mm timber, 1.2 m of 75 x 25 mm timber, 0.3 mm of 100 x 25 mm timber, 1.5 m of 19 x 12 mm moulding and 1.2 m of 20 x 19 mm timber. Dimensions: 320 mm long; 200 mm wide; 135 mm high.

Continue the lines over the edges 8 mm for the depth. Set a marking gauge to 8 mm, draw a line from the inside face across the ends of the side pieces and to the 15 mm lines. This allows for size or planing variations. Trace over the lines with a utility knife and cut the shoulder lines of the rebate to depth using a tenon saw. Place the side in the vice and pare down the rebate using a 25 mm bevelled-edge chisel and finish off the rebates with a router fitted with a 12 mm bit or a rebate plane. Repeat this process for all the side rebates.

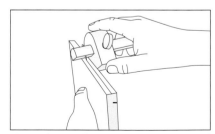

5 *Set the marking gauge to 8 mm and draw a line from the inside face across the ends of the pieces.*

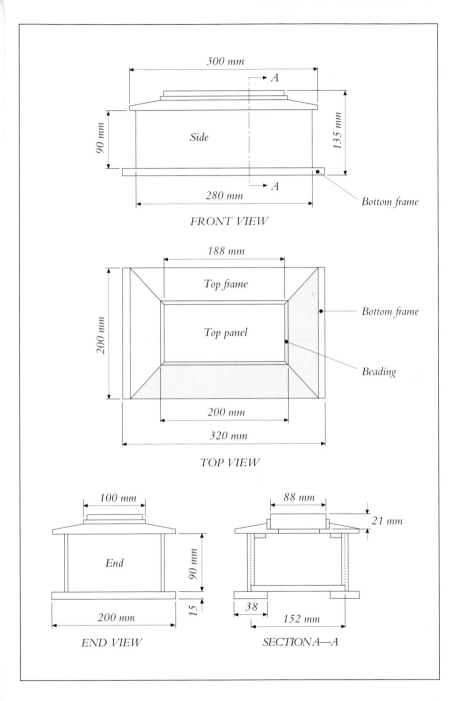

300 mm

→ A

90 mm

Side

135 mm

280 mm

→ A

Bottom frame

FRONT VIEW

188 mm

Top frame

Bottom frame

200 mm

Top panel

Beading

200 mm

320 mm

TOP VIEW

100 mm

88 mm

21 mm

End

90 mm

200 mm

15

38

152 mm

END VIEW

SECTION A—A

MAKING MITRES

A mitre joint can be hard to cut, but a mitre box to guide the saw at 45 degrees or a mitre saw, which has its own blade and can be set to exact angles, can make the task easier. Mitres cut by hand may need to be chiselled or planed to ensure a perfect fit.

6 Cut the rebates on the bottom edges of the sides and ends to a width equal to the base thickness (15 mm) and a depth of 8 mm using a rebate plane or a router.

7 Flush the faces of the base panel with a smoothing plane if necessary. Plane one long edge of the base straight and square, and use a marking gauge or combination square to mark the 152 mm width on the face side. Cut on the waste side of the lines with a panel saw or circular saw and plane the bottom panel to size with a smoothing plane. Mark off the 272 mm panel length, square the lines across, and trace over the lines with a utility knife. Cut the panel to length and plane the edges to the knife lines with a sharp, finely-set block plane.

ASSEMBLING THE BOX

8 Put the sides, ends and base together without adhesive to check the box is square. Check that the base fits and make any adjustments. Sand all inside faces with 180 grade abrasive paper.

9 On the outer face of the base panel, draw a line 6 mm from the edges. Mark drilling positions on the sides 80 mm in from the ends and centrally across the width on the ends. Drill 4 mm screw holes, angling them slightly to the outside, and countersink the holes.

10 Apply adhesive to the rebate faces on the side and end pieces and spread it evenly with your finger. With their bottom edges facing up, bring the sides and ends together. Place a quick-release cramp at each end and one from end to end, using scrap material between the clamps and the panels to protect the timber. Place the base in its rebates and square up the box. Drill 2 mm pilot holes in the box through the base. Insert six 20 mm ($^3/_4$ in) x No. 6 gauge countersink screws. Leave the box aside to dry.

THE TOP FRAME

11 Take a 1.2 m length of the 75 x 25 mm timber, plane one long narrow edge straight and square and use this face to mark a width of 66

13 Mark the bevel of the top face, cramp the timber over the edge of a work surface and plane the bevel.

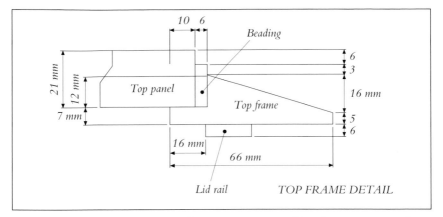

mm across both sides with a marking gauge. Carry the marks round the ends and plane to size using a smoothing plane.

12 Cut a rebate 16 mm wide and 12 mm deep on the inner edge of the top face with a router or plane.

13 From the bottom face, draw a line 5 mm along the outer edges to mark the bevel of the top face. Fasten the timber over the edge of a work surface and plane the bevel.

14 Mark the length of the frame ends and sides on the outer edge.

Use a combination square to draw mitres on the bottom face and return the lines over the edges. Continue the line up to and across the rebate and then join the line from the top of the bevel to the corner. Trace over the lines with a utility knife. Use a tenon saw with a mitre box, or a mitre saw to cut the mitres and, if necessary, plane back to the lines, regularly checking the joint fit.

15 Place some adhesive on the mitre faces and rub it in well. Apply a little more adhesive to the mitres and bring the parts together in a frame cramp. Make sure all the joint faces

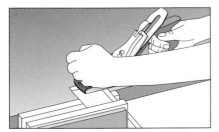

14 *Cut the mitres on the parts for the top frame and plane the mitres back to the knife lines.*

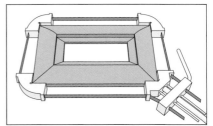

15 *Place some adhesive in the adjoining mitres and bring the top frame together in a frame cramp.*

are flush and remove any excess adhesive with a damp cloth.

THE BOTTOM FRAME

16 Take a 1.2 m length of 50 x 19 mm timber and plane one face side and one long edge straight and flat. Using a marking gauge, draw a line 38 mm from the edge along the length of the timber and plane to width with a smoothing plane. Mark off the length of the sides and ends, allowing space for mitres and saw cuts. Repeat the method described in steps 14 and 15 to join and finish the bottom frame.

MAKING THE BEADING

17 The beading for the lid (and top frame rail) is made from 19 x 12 mm moulding (finished size 15 x 6 mm). If another size has to be used, adjust the size of the top panel to suit.

18 Hold beading in place and mark the lengths. Mark the mitres on the ends and square the lines across the face sides. Trace over the lines with a utility knife and cut the mitres with a tenon saw. If necessary, trim the mitres carefully with a 25 mm chisel or a finely-set block plane.

FITTING THE TOP PANEL

19 Take the timber for the top panel and cut it roughly to length with a panel saw. Plane one side and end square. With the beading in place, use the top frame to mark the exact size of the top panel. Square the lines across the face of the top panel and

over the edges. Plane the panel to length and width, planing a slight bevel on the bottom edges to help with locating the panel in the frame.

20 Apply adhesive to the rebate in the top frame, to the edges of the top panel and to the sides and bottom edge of the beading. Assemble the whole of the lid, remove excess adhesive with a damp cloth and secure with quick-release cramps while the adhesive dries.

ASSEMBLING THE BOX

21 Shape the top outside edge of the bottom frame to a gentle curve by careful planing and sanding, or by using a round-over bit in a router.

22 Place the bottom frame on the bench and position the box evenly over the frame so that the overhang is equal on all sides. Mark the position of the box on the frame and set out the screw positions following the diagram on page 13: the holes must be centrally positioned for the side and end pieces of the box. Drill 4 mm pilot holes in the bottom frame and countersink the holes from underneath. Place the frame in position and drill 2 mm pilot holes in the box for the screws. Insert the six 25 mm (1 in) x No. 6 gauge countersunk screws and tighten.

23 Measure the inner dimensions of the box, reduce the size by 2 mm all round and draw a rectangle of this size centrally on the underside of the

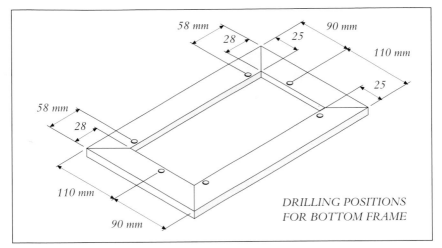

58 mm
28
25
90 mm
110 mm
25
58 mm
28
110 mm
90 mm

*DRILLING POSITIONS
FOR BOTTOM FRAME*

lid to position the lid rails. Take the 19 x 12 mm timber and mark the length of the lid rails, including mitres for the corners. Trace the lines with a utility knife before cutting the rails with a tenon saw. Fix the rails in place with 15 mm panel pins and punch the pins below the surface of the timber with a nail punch.

FINISHING

24 Remove the bottom frame from the box and sand all faces carefully with 180 grade abrasive paper. Use a damp cloth to dampen the surface of

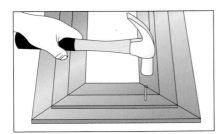

23 Fix the lid rails in place with 15 mm panel pins and punch the pins below the surface of the timber.

the timber lightly after the first sanding and allow it to dry before sanding all over with 240 grade paper. Use a cabinet scraper to remove any blemishes, bruises and scratches. Make good gaps with filler.

25 Apply a semi-gloss clear lacquer to finish the box. You may also use a water-based acrylic lacquer, but you must use an acrylic thinner to extend its drying time in hot weather as this will give you a better finish. Make sure you follow the manufacturer's instructions and use a good quality paintbrush. Apply a coat of lacquer to all the inside surfaces and leave to dry. Sand back with 240 grade abrasive paper and apply a second coat. Finish the inside faces before lacquering the outside. For a super-smooth finish, sand the exterior surface with very fine wet-and-dry abrasive paper, then with very fine grade steel wool. Dust well before applying the third coat of lacquer.

Jewellery box with beading

This beautiful box with a gabled lid and fine beading is a project for experienced woodworkers. It is made as one piece and then the lid is cut off to ensure a perfect match.

TOOLS

- Smoothing plane and block plane
- Rebate plane (or router and rebate bit)
- Hammer and nail punch
- Chisel: 6 mm, 25 mm
- Tenon saw
- Dovetail saw
- Jigsaw or coping saw
- Coping saw
- Tape measure or folding rule
- Combination square and pencil
- Utility knife and marking gauge
- Set of jeweller's screwdrivers
- Sliding bevel
- Cork sanding block
- Set square, compass and scissors
- Cabinet scraper (optional)
- Curved file and flat file
- Cramps: frame and quick-release
- Electric drill
- Mitre box or mitre saw
- Panel saw or circular saw
- Drill bits: 3 mm, countersunk

PREPARING THE BOX

1 The 16 mm timber should have a finished size of 12 mm when you buy it. Mark a face side and plane a face edge straight and square. Do not reduce the width to less than 130 mm.

2 From a 1.2 m length of timber, cut a 700 mm long piece for the sides and a 360 mm piece for the ends.

3 Mark out and plane the side timber to exactly 111 mm wide. Set out the sides and ends as per the diagrams on pages 16 and 18, making sure that the sides are going to match up with the ends. Remember that the whole box is made as one item and divided into two separate pieces later.

4 Mark the mitre lines across the edges of the sides and ends and trace over the lines with a utility knife to cut the cross-grain fibres. Place each panel in a vice and cut the mitres with a tenon saw. If the saw blade is not deep enough, turn over the panel and cut from the other edge. Plane back the mitres to the lines using a block plane. Repeat for each mitre and check the fit of the joints.

5 Cut the gables on the top edges of the ends with a tenon saw and plane back to the lines where the beading will be fixed.

6 Cramp each side piece firmly to a work surface and cut rebates on the top edges 8 mm wide and 6 mm

This jewellery box was made from sycamore, a warm honey-coloured wood, with contrasting dark hard wood used for the beading and the feet. The fine brass hinges and a jewellery box hasp are evocative of times past.

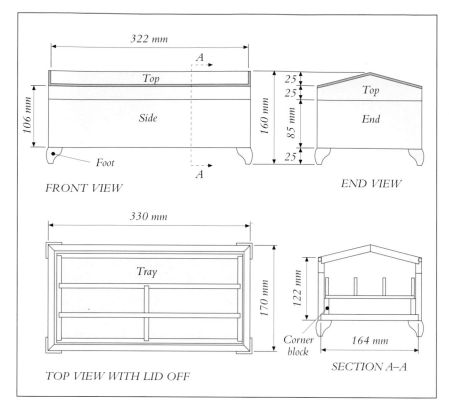

deep. Repeat for the gables of the end pieces, cutting the rebates 8 mm wide and 8 mm deep. Cut rebates 12 mm wide and 8 mm deep on the bottom edges of the sides and ends to take the base. Check all the corners meet exactly and number the joints for easy reference. Use a rebate plane or a router fitted with a rebating bit to cut the rebates.

6 Cut the rebates 12 mm wide and 8 mm deep on the bottom edge of the timber for the sides and ends.

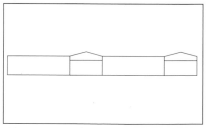

10 Lay out the parts with the face sides up and the joints well aligned. Secure each joint with masking tape.

MATERIALS*

PART	MATERIAL	LENGTH	NO.
Box sides	150 x 16 mm timber PAR	330 mm	2
Box ends	150 x 16 mm timber PAR	170 mm	2
Box base	100 x 16 mm timber PAR	322 mm	2
Box top	100 x 16 mm timber PAR	322 mm	2
Beading (sides)	9 x 9 mm moulding	330 mm	2
Beading (ends)	9 x 9 mm moulding	90 mm	4
Feet	32 x 25 mm timber PAR	25 mm	8
Corner blocks	125 x 10 mm timber PAR	30 mm	4
Tray sides	35 x 6 mm prepared ramin	307 mm	2
Tray ends	35 x 6 mm prepared ramin	143 mm	2
Tray divisions (long)	35 x 6 mm prepared ramin	299 mm	2
Tray division (cross)	35 x 6 mm prepared ramin	92 mm	1
Tray bottom	6 mm plywood	303 mm	2

OTHER: PVA adhesive; 25 mm wide masking tape; epoxy resin adhesive; six 20 mm (3/4 in) x No. 4 gauge countersunk wood screws (cross-head or slotted); eight 15 mm panel pins; eight 13 mm (1/2 in) x No. 0 gauge countersunk brass wood screws (cross-head or slotted); abrasive paper: one sheet of 120 grade, two sheets of 180, 240 and 600 grade wet-and-dry; 000 grade steel wool; two 25 mm brass butt hinges; jewellery box hasp, staple and fixings; lacquer

* Timber sizes are nominal. For timber types and sizes, see page 5. Finished dimensions (without feet): length 330 mm; width 170 mm; height 135 mm.

7 Take the 100 x 16 mm timber and cut two 340 mm boards for the base. Plane an edge of each board straight and make sure the face sides are flush. Put adhesive on the joining edges, bring the boards together and apply two quick-release cramps. Put the base panel aside to dry.

8 Cut two 340 mm pieces from the 100 x 16 mm timber for the top. Set the sliding bevel to the angle of the end gables and transfer this angle to the meeting edges of the top boards. Plane the meeting edges of the top boards to this angle with a smoothing plane, checking the fit often. Sand the inside faces of all the panels with abrasive paper.

ASSEMBLING THE BOX

9 Remove the cramps from the base and check the face side is flush. Plane a long edge square with a smoothing

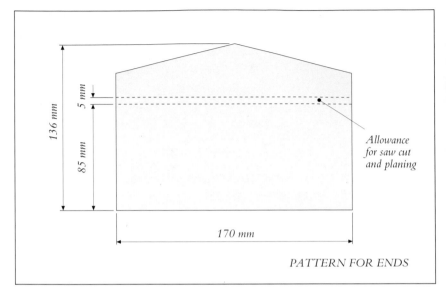

136 mm

5 mm

85 mm

Allowance for saw cut and planing

170 mm

PATTERN FOR ENDS

plane. Square one end and trace over the line with a utility knife. Then plane the end square.

10 Lay out the parts with the face sides up and the mitre joints well aligned. Secure each joint with a piece of masking tape on the outside from top to bottom and three shorter pieces at 90 degrees to the first. Assemble the box into its upright form and check that it is square.

11 Mark the size of the box frame on the base and make sure it is square. Cut the base with a saw and plane to finished size to fit in the rebates in the sides and ends. Draw a line 5 mm from all edges and mark the screw positions: on the sides 85 mm from the ends and on the ends, centrally across the width. Drill the 3 mm clearance holes and countersink

them. Check the fit of the pieces and adjust if necessary.

12 Put adhesive on the mitres of the sides and ends and join the parts. Use masking tape to secure the final joint and apply a frame cramp. Make sure the rebates finish flush. Turn the box over, prop it up with scrap material, and put the base in position, but do not attach it at this stage.

FITTING THE TOP
13 Mark the length of the two top pieces. Trace over the lines with a utility knife and cut with a tenon saw. Plane back the pieces carefully to the lines, working from the ends towards the centre to avoid chipping out the end grain.

14 Set a sliding bevel to the angle required for joining the top boards to

the sides. Hold the pieces in position and mark the width at the ends. Set a marking gauge to the width and draw lines along the length of both pieces. Plane to width and the correct bevel angle, checking the fit.

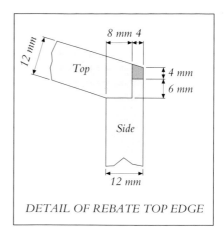

15 The inside face of each board has to be bevelled at 90 degrees to the angle on the outside edges so the top sits flat in the side rebates. Remove the base from the box and hold the top boards in place. Turn over the box and mark the rebate width on the inside faces of boards. Square a line to the outer edge and mark the angle. Plane the angle on the inside faces, checking the fit often.

DETAIL OF REBATE TOP EDGE

16 Apply adhesive in the rebates and attach the base with 20 mm ($^3/4$ in) x No. 4 gauge countersunk screws. Apply adhesive to the top rebates and the joining edges of the top boards. Insert the top boards, place light weights on them to ensure they stay flat and put the box aside to dry.

FITTING THE BEADING

17 You can buy beading already finished in a variety of sizes. Choose one in a contrasting hardwood closest to the finished size (9 x 9 mm for example); it will be planed to size after it has been glued in place. Mark the two squarest adjacent sides to fit in the rebate.

18 Hold the beading in the side rebates with the marked faces to the outside, mark the inner lengths and

square the lines. Mark the mitres outwards on the marked faces. Trace over the lines with a knife and cut the mitres with a tenon saw. A mitre box will make this task easier.

19 Mark and cut the beading for the ends in a similar way, except that the vertical mitre lines should be marked using a sliding bevel. Make sure you align the joints carefully. For final fitting, use a sharp 25 mm chisel to pare off any excess beading. If the fit is not perfect, the finish of the job will be affected so always cut new pieces rather than try to force pieces to fit. Number each piece and its position before glueing and taping all the beading into place.

20 When the adhesive dries, remove the masking tape and plane with a smoothing plane the beading so it is nearly flush. Repeat on the ends. Lastly, use a cabinet scraper or 120 grade abrasive paper to flush the beading and then put the box aside.

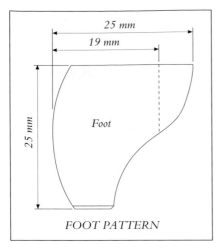

25 mm

19 mm

25 mm

Foot

FOOT PATTERN

MAKING THE FEET

21 Take the 32 x 25 mm timber and plane to a width of 25 mm and a thickness of 19 mm. Mark eight 25 mm sections on the 25 mm wide face, leaving 5 mm between them for the saw cuts. Two sections form each foot so make sure the timber grain matches where possible. Square the lines across the face and mark the mitres on the joining edges of each pair. Trace over the lines with a utility knife, cramp the timber in a vice and cut the mitres with a tenon saw and mitre box or a mitre saw.

22 Place adhesive on the mitres and join the pairs to make each foot, using masking tape to hold the joints until the adhesive sets. Use a compass or small round objects to draw a cardboard template of the foot shape (see the pattern above). Trace the template on the outer face of each foot. Place each foot in a vice and cut with a jigsaw or a coping saw.

Use a round file to finish the inner curves, and a flat file for the outer curves. Plane the outer face of each foot, working away from the mitre to avoid chipping the adjoining block. Using a sanding block and 120 grade abrasive paper, sand the face of each foot.

CUTTING THE LID

23 Set out the cutting marks on the box ends 85 mm and 90 mm from the bottom and set a marking gauge to these lines. Draw lines along both sides with the marking gauge resting on the bottom edge. Secure the box in a portable vice and carefully cut the sides with a panel saw or circular saw set to a cutting depth of 14 mm. Use a panel saw to cut the box ends as the slower cutting action reduces the chance of chipping when cutting across the grain. Plane the rough saw marks on the box with a smoothing plane. Place the lid in a vice or put packing under the sloping faces and clamp it to a work surface so it is level before planing its cut edge. Check that the lid fits on the box properly and adjust if necessary.

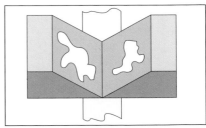

22 Place adhesive on the mitres and join the pairs to make each foot using masking tape to hold the joint.

PREPARING THE TRAY

24 Measure the inside of the box and, if necessary, adjust the tray measurements to fit. The tray is 3 mm shorter and 7 mm narrower than the inside of the box. You will also have to adjust the internal dimensions of the tray if the moulding you use is other than 35 x 6 mm ramin.

25 For the tray bottom, straighten and square one edge of the plywood with a block plane. Square a line across one end. Mark off the length of the tray bottom and square another line across and finally mark the fourth line for width. Trace along all the lines with a utility knife, cut the plywood slightly oversize with a tenon saw and use a sharp block plane to bring it back to the marked lines and to get the edges neat and square.

26 Cut the components for the tray from the prepared 35 x 6 mm ramin: the sides should be 307 mm long the ends 143 mm, the dividers 199 mm and the cross dividers 92 mm. For each saw cut, use a square to mark the cutting line, trace along the marked line with a utility knife, use a tenon saw to make the cut and asharp, finely-set block plane to trim back to the cutting line and to get the ends square.

27 On the bottom edges of the tray sides and ends, cut rebates 6 mm wide and 4 mm deep to take the base. Plane back the rebates on each of the four pieces.

28 Use an end piece to mark the rebate width for joining the sides by holding the end flush with the length mark on the sides. Square the line across the inner face of the side and continue it over the edges. Mark the positions of the housing joints on the ends (to take the dividers) using the same technique.

29 Use a marking gauge to mark the 4 mm rebate depth on the edges of the sides and then mark the 2 mm depth of the housing joints on the top and bottom edges of the ends. Lay out the parts and check the joints line up before tracing over the marking lines with a utility knife.

30 Holding the side firmly in a portable work bench, cut the rebate depth with a dovetail saw. Cramp the side to a work surface and remove the waste with a 25 mm chisel. Repeat for all rebates. Cut the housing joints in the same way, but use a 6 mm chisel to remove the waste. Square the ends of the divisions and the tray ends using a block plane.

ASSEMBLING THE TRAY

31 Mark the position of the cross piece centrally on the dividers and one side. Mark out the positions of the housing joints and also mark the central halving joint to the 6 mm thickness of the material. Square the

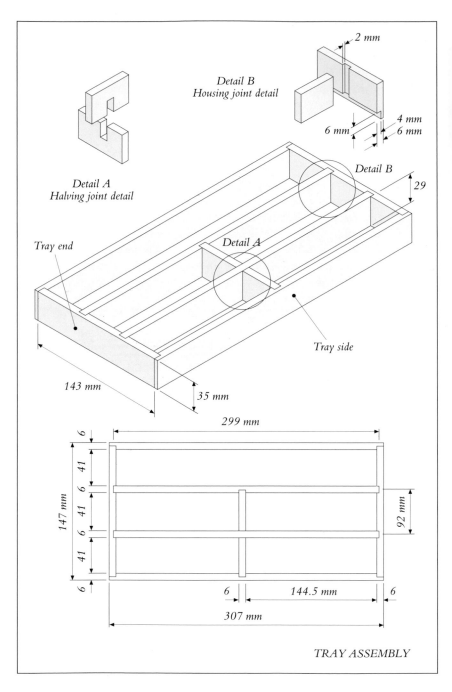

2 mm

Detail B
Housing joint detail

4 mm
6 mm

6 mm

Detail A
Halving joint detail

Detail B

29

Tray end

Detail A

Tray side

143 mm

35 mm

299 mm

6

41

147 mm

6

41

6

41

6

92 mm

6

144.5 mm

6

307 mm

TRAY ASSEMBLY

lines over the edges and trace with a utility knife. Cut the joints with a dovetail saw. Remove the waste with a 6 mm chisel. Try a dry fit of the parts, using cramps to hold the tray together, and make any adjustments. Square the end of the cross piece using a block plane.

32 Square one edge and one end of the tray bottom with the smoothing plane. Measure the rebated box opening, transfer the size to the tray bottom and cut and plane the bottom to size. Make sure the tray will finish square and fit in the box. Take the tray apart and sand the parts with abrasive paper: first with 180 grade, then 240 grade. Practise assembling the tray before applying adhesive to the joints. Assemble the tray and use two quick-release cramps to hold the tray together. Make sure the ends are pushed firmly into the side rebates. Apply adhesive to the base rebates, attach the tray base and place weights on it to keep it flat while the adhesive dries. If the ends loosen, nail in some 15 mm panel pins through the ends into the sides to help secure the fastening.

33 When the glue is dry, carefully sand all the joints. Fit the tray and adjust with a smoothing plane if necessary. Cut four 9 x 9 mm corner blocks 30 mm long to keep the tray raised off the bottom of the box and to strengthen the joints. Sand the pieces well and glue them into place in the corners of the box.

FINISHING

34 Measure 50 mm from the ends along the hinging edge of the box and square the lines across. Hold a hinge in place on the inside of the line, mark the leaf length and square another line. Repeat for the other hinge. Align the lid with the box and carefully transfer the hinge marks. Set the marking gauge from the centre of the pin to the outside of the leaf and mark this depth on both the box and the lid between the hinge marks.

35 Carefully remove the waste from the hinge recesses on the lid and box with a 25 mm chisel. Place a hinge on the box and use a fine panel pin to create a pilot hole for the No. 0 gauge screw. Insert a screw using a jeweller's screwdriver. Repeat for the other hinge. Align the lid, mark the screw positions from the hinges, make pilot holes and insert a screw in each hinge. Test the lid and make any adjustments before fixing the hinges permanently. Fit the hasp and staple catch on the front.

36 Remove the hardware. Turn the box upside down and attach the feet using a small amount of epoxy resin adhesive. Leave to dry overnight.

37 Sand all surfaces really well with 180 grade abrasive paper. If necessary, punch any pin heads below the surface and fill any gaps with wood filler. Sand the box with 240 grade abrasive paper before applying two coats of lacquer.

Painted toy box on castors

This painted toy box with curved edges is a quick weekend project. It is made from MDF and decorated with a simple stencil motif. Swivel castors make it very easy to move around.

MATERIALS★

PART	MATERIAL	LENGTH	WIDTH	No.
Base	15 mm MDF	700 mm	500 mm	1
Sides	15 mm MDF	650 mm	385 mm	2
Ends	15 mm MDF	420 mm	320 mm	2
Cleats	25 mm scotia moulding	319 mm		4

OTHER: PVA adhesive; four small swivel castors; eight 40 mm chipboard screws; sixteen 13 mm (1/2 in) x No. 6 gauge countersunk screws (cross-head or slotted); twenty 40 mm panel pins; abrasive paper: one sheet of 100 grade and one sheet of 240 grade; cardboard; acrylic-based paint; primer/sealer; wood filler; masking tape

★ Finished dimensions: length 700 mm; width 500 mm; height 416 mm.

PREPARING THE BOARDS

1 Using a tape measure, combination square and straight-edge, mark the parts on the MDF, leaving a 5 mm allowance for saw cuts. Check that the parts are square.

2 Cut the parts on the waste side of the lines, using a circular saw and a straight-edge clamped to the board. Pin the matching pieces together with panel pins and plane the edges straight and square back to the lines.

SHAPING THE TOP EDGE

3 Square a line down the centre of the side face. On the cardboard, draw a 325 x 125 mm rectangle (make sure it is squared) and inside it draw a curved shape to be used as a half template. Cut out the template. Line up the template with the centre line of the sides. Trace around the template, flip it over, and trace the shape on the other side.

3 Trace around the template, flip it over, and trace the shape on the other side of the centre line.

This movable box on castors has many uses, but is especially handy for storing toys. The design is very adaptable—alter the height or size of the box to suit your needs—and the box can be decorated in various ways.

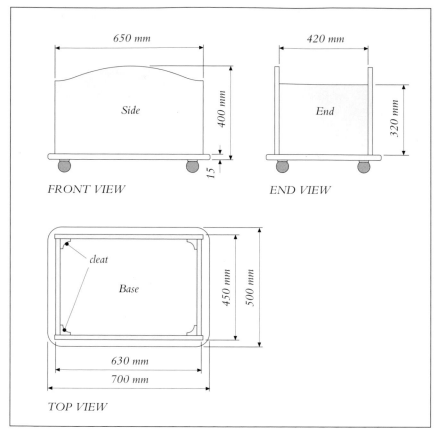

650 mm

400 mm

Side

FRONT VIEW

420 mm

320 mm

End

END VIEW

15

cleat

Base

450 mm

500 mm

630 mm

700 mm

TOP VIEW

4 Keeping the sides pinned, cut the top edges with a coping saw or jigsaw. Use spokeshaves or a sanding block and 100 grade abrasive paper to smooth the curved top. Draw a line 17.5 mm from either end and continue the lines over the edges. Carefully separate the pinned pieces.

ASSEMBLING THE BOX

5 Start three panel pins evenly spaced on the 17.5 mm line. Put adhesive on the edge of an end panel. Apply a little more adhesive and line up the joint, making sure the guide line on top matches the centre of the edge of the end. Drive the nails in. Attach the other end. Turn the box around and attach the second side in the same manner. Keep the bottom edges flush.

6 Nail a piece of timber diagonally across the bottom of the box to keep it square while the adhesive sets.

7 Use a round object to draw the round corners on the base. Cut the

TOOLS

- Smoothing plane
- Circular saw
- Tape measure and straight-edge
- Combination square and pencil
- Coping saw or jigsaw
- Hammer
- Spokeshaves: round-bottom and flat-bottom
- Electric drill
- Drill bits: 2 mm, 3 mm, 5 mm, countersink bit
- Utility knife and scissors
- Cork sanding block or electric sander
- Screwdriver (cross-head or slotted)

corners with a coping saw or jigsaw, and smooth them over with a sanding block and abrasive paper.

8 Draw lines 32.5 mm from the sides of the base for the screws. Mark a screw hole in the centre of the end and measure 250 mm either side of it for two more screws. Draw lines 42.5 mm in from the ends and mark a screw hole in the centre. Drill 5 mm holes and countersink.

9 Remove the brace and place the frame with the bottom edge facing up. Prop it into position. Align the bottom panel and make 3 mm pilot holes in the bottom edge of the frame. Attach the bottom panel to the frame with 40 mm chipboard screws. Turn the box right way up.

10 Cut the four cleats, sand the exposed ends and glue the cleats in place. Use masking tape to hold them while the adhesive dries.

11 Place the box face down on a work surface and draw a guide line 50 mm from the edges of the base. Hold a castor in place, drill a 2 mm pilot hole and attach the castor with 13 mm (1/2 in) x No. 6 gauge screws. Repeat for each castor.

FINISHING
12 Apply one coat of primer or sealer and at least two coats of paint. Sand lightly between coats with 240 grade abrasive paper. Enlarge the stencil design on page 64 with a photocopier or choose your own design and decorate the box.

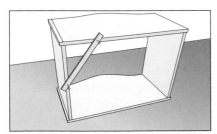

6 Nail a piece of timber diagonally across the bottom of the box to keep it square while the adhesive dries.

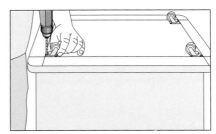

11 Place the box face down and, holding a castor in place, drill a 2 mm hole and attach the castor.

Inspired by old-fashioned treasure caskets, this chest has classic fittings and handles. Here, pine was chosen for the construction, but any quality solid timber would be equally effective. The chest is finished with teak oil.

Traditional chest with curved lid

This sturdy chest is ideal for storage as well as being a decorative piece. The web-and-cooper construction of the curved lid is a traditional technique that takes a little patience to finish well.

TOOLS

- Jack plane and smoothing plane
- Jigsaw
- Dowelling jig
- Tenon saw, panel saw or circular saw
- Orbital sander
- Combination square and sliding bevel
- Utility knife
- Marking gauge
- Electric drill
- Drill bits: 8 mm and 8 mm plug cutter, 5 mm, 3 mm, countersink
- Screwdriver (cross-head or slotted)
- Hammer
- Three 900 mm sash cramps
- Chisel
- Flat-bottom spokeshave
- Mitre box or mitre saw

PREPARING THE BOARDS

1 The 200 x 25 mm timber should have a finished size of 193 x 21 mm. You need two 710 mm boards for the front and back, three 410 mm boards for each end and two 680 mm boards for the base. Cut the boards with a panel or circular saw. Straighten the long edges with a jack plane. Using a combination square, check the board edges are square.

2 Arrange the six boards for the front, back and base into three adjacent panels, face sides up, and position an arrowhead mark across the face of the boards. Arrange the six boards for the two ends in a similar way.

3 On the joining edges of the boards for the front, back and bottom, find the centre and square a line across. Measure out 150 mm from either side of the centre, then 300 mm, and square the lines across so you have five dowel positions 150 mm apart. Mark the dowel positions on the three end boards in the same manner. For each end, the first two boards have three dowel holes set 150 mm apart and the third has two dowel holes 100 mm on each side of the centre.

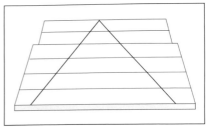

2 Arrange the boards into the panels, face sides up, and place an arrowhead mark across the face of the boards.

MATERIALS★

Part	Material	Finished length	No.
Front	200 x 25 mm timber PAR	700 mm	2
Back	200 x 25 mm timber PAR	700 mm	2
Ends	200 x 25 mm timber PAR	400 mm	6
Base	200 x 25 mm timber PAR	658 mm	2
Lid	125 x 25 mm timber PAR	655 mm	6
Lid ends	225 x 25 mm timber PAR	400 mm	2
Hinge rails	225 x 25 mm timber offcuts	613 mm	2
Skirting (sides)	100 x 25 mm timber PAR	742 mm	2
Skirting (ends)	100 x 25 mm timber PAR	442 mm	2

OTHER: PVA adhesive; abrasive paper: two sheets each of 100 grade and 320 grade, three sheets of 180 grade; forty 38 mm (1 1/2 in) x No. 8 gauge countersunk wood screws; ten 32 mm (1 1/4 in) x No. 8 gauge countersunk wood screws; two 20 mm (3/4 in) x No. 6 gauge round-head screws with washers; 30 mm panel pins; two strap hinges with fixings; one hasp and staple with fixings; 300 mm fine chain; two box handles; twenty-eight 40 x 8 mm timber dowels; lacquer; teak oil; very fine grade steel wool

★ Timber sizes given are nominal. For timber types and sizes, see page 5.
Finished dimensions: length 742 mm; width 442 mm; height 550 mm.

4 Set a marking gauge to 10.5 mm and draw a line along the joining edge of each board to mark the centres of the dowel holes.

5 Put each board in a vice, set the dowelling jig from the face side and drill the dowel holes 21 mm deep.

6 Reorganise the boards into panels and, working on one panel at a time, spread adhesive on the joining edge of one board and in the holes. Tap in the dowels with a hammer. Spread adhesive on the edge of the next board and bring the boards together.

Put scrap timber between the three panels and the sash cramps and tighten the cramps until the adhesive oozes out. If you over-tighten the cramps, the boards will buckle. If needed, place a third cramp over the top of the panel with a block under it to keep the panel flat. Clean off any excess adhesive and repeat for the end panel.

7 When the front, back and bottom are dry, straighten a long edge on each. Mark the length of each panel and square lines across. Trace over the lines with a utility knife and cut

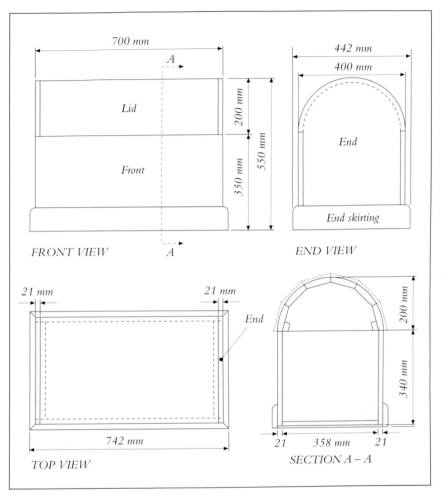

FRONT VIEW

END VIEW

TOP VIEW

SECTION A – A

the panel to length. If using a circular saw, cramp a batten to the board to guide the saw.

8 Mark the width of the front, back and bottom and cut each panel slightly over width. Straighten and square the edges with a jack plane. Put the panels aside, but keep the offcuts for the hinge rails.

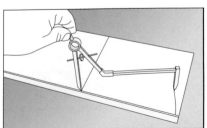

9 **Cut two 410 mm boards for the lid. Find the centre of the board and draw a semi-circle with a 179 mm radius.**

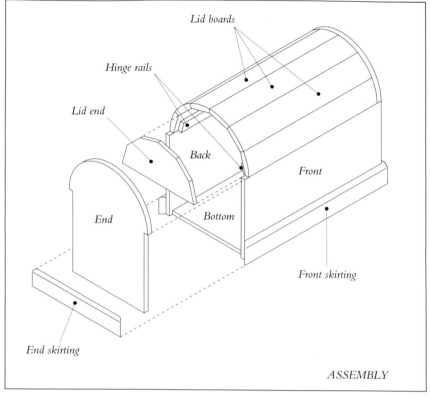

Lid boards

Hinge rails

Lid end

Back

Front

End

Bottom

Front skirting

Front skirting

End skirting

ASSEMBLY

MAKING THE LID

9 Cut two 410 mm boards for the lid ends. Find the centre of the board width and square a line across. Use a compass to draw a semi-circle with a 179 mm radius. Working from the centre line, use a 60/30 set square to mark angles as shown in the diagram. Draw lines from the central point to each point and join the points where the angle lines meet the semi-circle.

10 Temporarily nail the lid ends together with 30 mm pins. Use a jigsaw to cut them roughly to shape and plane both pieces back to size.

11 On the 125 x 25 mm timber, mark the lengths for the lid boards, leaving a 5 mm gap between each one. Cut out each board with a panel saw and leave them all slightly over length at this stage. Clamp the boards together in a vice and plane them to a thickness of 105 mm using a jack plane. Plane both edges so that they are true. Set a sliding bevel to 75 degrees, mark the angle on the joining edges of the boards and continue the lines over the edges. Place each board in a vice and carefully bevel one edge with a plane. Don't bevel both edges yet.

12 Using the lid ends, mark the inner width of each board (they may vary slightly) and gauge a line down the length of the board. Plane the bevel on the other joining edge of each board, checking the fit with the lid end. Do not plane the top boards to width until they are finally fitted.

13 Measure 10 mm from the end lines of each board and square lines across. Find the centre of the width and mark the screw position on the line. Drill 8 mm plug holes 6 mm deep. Change to a 5 mm drill bit and drill the boards right through.

14 Take one lid end and put adhesive on the lowest section on either side. Attach the boards with screws. Then attach these boards to the other lid end. Make sure the bevelled edges match the first angle on the lid ends, allowing any extra board to protrude beyond the lid end if necessary. Clean off any excess adhesive. Dry fit the next boards on either side and make any adjustments before attaching them in the same manner. Plane the bevels on the top

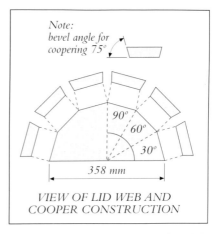

Note:
bevel angle for coopering 75°

90°
60°
30°

358 mm

VIEW OF LID WEB AND COOPER CONSTRUCTION

two boards to fit exactly and attach them. Ensure all screw heads are well below the board surfaces.

SHAPING THE END PANELS

15 Plane the bottom of the end panels straight and square. On each panel, square a line up the centre. From the bottom, measure 340 mm and square a line across. On this line, draw a semi-circle with a radius of 200 mm. Mark a point on the line 21 mm from where the semi-circle meets it and, from each of these points, square a line to the bottom, around the edge and back up the

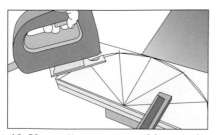

10 Use a jigsaw to roughly cut the shape of the lid ends and plane them to size with a smoothing plane.

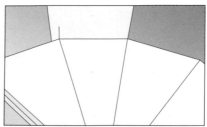

12 From the lid ends, mark the inner width of each board and square a line down the length of the board.

other side. Trace over the straight lines with a utility knife.

16 Carefully cut the curved top with a jigsaw. Then cut the indented sides. Plane back the edges to the knife lines using a smoothing plane. Use a sharp chisel to pare back the corners.

ASSEMBLING THE CHEST
17 At each end of the front panel, mark a screw hole 50 mm from the top, then three more holes 80 mm apart, the last being 50 mm from the base. Find the centre of the base edge, mark two screw holes 250 mm on either side of it, then measure out another 250 mm for two more holes. Repeat for the back. On the ends, find the centre of the bottom edge and mark two screw holes 125 mm on either side of it. Check the panels and holes line up exactly and make any adjustments. Drill 8 mm plug holes, 6 mm deep. Use a 5 mm drill bit to drill the holes right through.

18 Put adhesive on the end of the base and bring the end panel into contact with it. Align the panels.

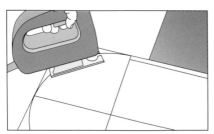

16 Carefully cut the curved top with a jigsaw. Then cut the indented sides. Plane back the panel to the lines.

Drill 3 mm pilot holes in the base and attach the end with 38 mm (1½ in) No. 8 screws. Clean off the excess adhesive. Then attach the other end and the front and back. Make sure the panels are square. If necessary, flush the front and back to the ends with a smoothing plane.

ATTACHING THE SKIRTING
19 Take the skirting timber, hold it against the chest front and mark the length on the skirting including the mitres. Draw mitres on the edges and across both faces. Trace the lines with a knife, before cutting with a tenon saw. Repeat for all skirting. Check the mitres match, and plane if necessary. Use a smoothing plane to round over the top edges.

20 Draw a line 40 mm up from the bottom edge around the entire box. On the front and back, find the centre and measure out 250 mm on either side for the screw holes. On the ends, mark the centre. Drill the 5 mm screw holes and countersink the holes on the inside of the box.

21 Lay the box on its side and draw a line 85 mm up from the bottom on the ends. Apply adhesive to the box and attach the skirting, lining up the top edge with the 85 mm line. Fix the skirting with 32 mm (1¼ in) No. 8 wood screws.

FITTING THE LID
22 Use a sharp spokeshave to round the ends of the box to the lines.

Work from the top of the curve down the sides, not upwards as the spokeshave will dig in. Then plane the ends of the lid boards flush with the lid ends and check the lid fits between the ends of the box.

23 Cut the hinge rails from the offcuts, glue them to the inside bottom edges of the lid and cramp into place. Plane the rails flush once the adhesive has set.

24 Sit the lid in position and copy the shape of the chest ends on the lid ends. Remove the lid and secure it to a portable work bench. Plane the lid to a round shape, following the grain, and check the fit often. Finish with an orbital sander and 100 grade abrasive paper. Remove flat spots by sanding across the grain, but be sure to finish by sanding with the grain.

FINISHING THE BOX

25 Bend one leaf of each strap hinge to match the curved shape of the top. Attach the hinges on the outside of the back, 90 mm in from each end and at 90 degrees to the hinging

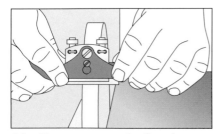

22 Use a curved flat-bottom spokeshave to round the ends of the box back to the lines.

Instead of rounding over the top edges of the skirting for this chest, you may choose to plane a simple 10 mm chamfer with a smoothing plane. Alternatively, buy skirting that has been pre-moulded.

edge. Attach the hasp and staple or use a similar latch. Mark the position of the chest handles below the curved top of the ends to prevent the internal fixings from catching on the lid ends and attach the handles. Using two 20 mm ($^3/_4$ in) x No. 6 gauge round-head screws with washers, attach one end of the chain inside the box on the centre line of the lid end, about 100 mm up from the bottom edge. Fix the other end of the chain to the inside face of the chest end, about 30 mm below the face edge height.

26 Finish the screw holes with plugs made by using an 8 mm plug cutter on off-cuts of the chest timber, trying to match the grain of the chest. Use a smoothing plane to flush the plugs to the surface of the chest after they have been glued in and the adhesive has set.

27 Remove the fittings and the lid. Fill any holes or gaps and steam out bruises with a damp cloth and hot iron. Sand the chest inside and out, finishing by hand. Apply two coats of lacquer. Use very fine steel wool to rub two coats of teak oil in the grain.

Sewing chest with upholstered lid

This versatile chest has a tray attached with a hinge and pivot bars, and a front panel that folds down for easy access. Once the pieces are cut to size, this project is quick and easy to assemble.

PREPARATION

1 Mark the main chest parts on the 15 mm MDF using a tape measure, pencil and a straight-edge for the larger pieces and a combination square and pencil for the smaller ones. Leave a 5 mm space between each piece for the saw cuts. Check the pieces are square by measuring the diagonals. With a straight batten cramped to the board to guide the saw, cut the parts a little over size

and use a smoothing plane to bring them to finished sizes. Plane the edges straight and square.

2 Set out the screw holes using a combination square to draw lines 7.5 mm from the edge along the sides and bottom of the back panel and along the bottom of the ends. On the bottom of the back, mark screw holes 70 mm from either end, then 187 mm. On the sides of the back, mark screw holes 50 mm from the top and bottom edges, and one centrally. On the bottom of the end panels, mark screw holes centrally and 50 mm from both ends. Drill the 5 mm clearance holes and countersink them. On the base, draw lines 21 mm from the back and sides to mark the positions of the back feet. For the front feet, draw lines 21 mm from the sides and 35 mm from the front. Then drill and countersink 5 mm clearance holes for the screws.

ASSEMBLING THE CHEST

3 Attach the ends to the base with PVA adhesive and 40 mm chipboard screws. If you nail the joint together first to make attaching the ends easier, punch the panel pins below the surface and fill the holes when

You can make this chest a much easier project by having the materials cut to size when you purchase them. The upholstery work is easily done at home, but you may choose to have the fabric fitted by a professional upholsterer.

MATERIALS*

Part	Material	Length	Width	No.
Lid	15 mm MDF	748 mm	408 mm	1
Front flap	15 mm MDF	700 mm	270 mm	1
Ends	15 mm MDF	330 mm	270 mm	2
Back	15 mm MDF	700 mm	270 mm	1
Base	15 mm MDF	670 mm	327 mm	1
Tray sides	9 mm MDF	646 mm	50 mm	2
Tray ends	9 mm MDF	232 mm	50 mm	2
Tray divider	9 mm MDF	626 mm	50 mm	1
Tray divider	9 mm MDF	232 mm	50 mm	1
Tray bottom	9 mm MDF	646 mm	250 mm	1
Pivot bars	9 mm MDF	118 mm	25 mm	2
Hinge rail	9 mm MDF	640 mm	35 mm	1
Cleats	25 x 25 mm PAR	320 mm	21 mm	2

OTHER: PVA adhesive; sixty 16 mm (5/8 in) x No. 4 gauge countersunk wood screws (cross-head or slotted); sixteen 40 mm chipboard screws; two 25 mm (1 in) x No. 6 gauge countersunk screws; four washers; seven (1 1/4 in) x No. 8 gauge countersunk wood screws; sixteen 30 mm panel pins; fourteen 20 mm (3/4 in) x No. 6 gauge countersunk wood screws; two 38 x 8 mm timber dowels; dowel centre points; four timber ball feet, 60 x 75 mm in diameter; contact adhesive; wood filler; abrasive paper: 180 and 240 grade; 1500 mm piano hinge; two 50 mm butt hinges and screws; one gripper catch and fixings (or magnetic catch); 750 x 410 mm foam; upholstery tacks (or staple gun with 10 mm staples); 900 x 550 mm fabric (allow for pattern); 2400 mm braiding

* Finished dimensions for this chest are: length 750 mm; width 410 mm; height 380 mm.

finishing. Then attach the back panel to the ends and base.

4 On the front edge of both ends, mark a dowel position 40 mm from the top edge and in the centre of the edge. Drill an 8 mm hole to a depth of 30 mm. Pilot two matching holes on the inner face of the front flap and drill them to a depth of 10 mm. Insert dowels into the ends (with just a little adhesive) and check that the front will sit flush.

5 Turn the chest upside down with the front in position. Cut the piano hinge to length with a hacksaw, file smooth and lay it across the bottom

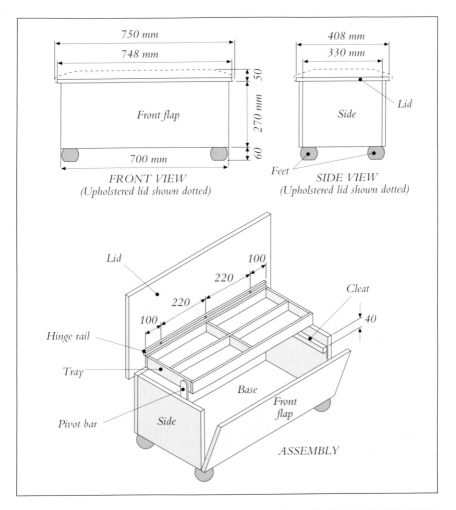

750 mm
748 mm
50
270 mm
60

Front flap

700 mm

FRONT VIEW
(Upholstered lid shown dotted)

408 mm
330 mm

Side

Lid

Feet

SIDE VIEW
(Upholstered lid shown dotted)

Lid
100
220
220
Cleat
100
40
Hinge rail
Tray
Base
Front flap
Pivot bar   Side

ASSEMBLY

of the chest and front flap. Centre the knuckle over the joint. Drill 2 mm pilot holes for the 16 mm (⁵/₈ in) x No. 4 gauge screws. Insert only enough screws to hold the front in place temporarily.

6 On the sides, draw a line 79 mm from the top to mark the position of the support cleats. Fold the front

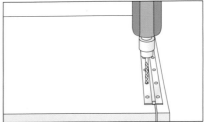

5 Turn the chest upside down, centre the hinge and attach with enough screws to hold the front temporarily.

down and measure 7 mm in from the front edge of the sides to position the front of the cleats. Mark and cut the cleats from 25 x 25 mm timber. Drill two 5 mm clearance holes in each cleat, 50 mm from either end. Countersink the holes. Attach with 32 mm (1¹/₂ in) x No. 8 gauge countersunk screws, together with some PVA adhesive.

7 Attach the four ball feet to the base of the box using four 38 mm (1 in) x No. 8 countersunk gauge screws and a little PVA adhesive.

8 On the top edge of the back, measure 75 mm from the sides and square a line across the edge. Hold a hinge in place, mark the length and square another line across. Continue the lines a few millimetres down the outside back. Set a marking gauge to slightly less than the thickness of a hinge knuckle (no more than 1 mm) and draw a line on the outside back between the two hinge lines. Cut the hinge recess on the inside of the lines with a tenon saw and remove the waste with a 25 mm chisel. Attach

the hinges so the leaf is flush with the back inside face and the hinge knuckle is set a few millimetres away from the chest.

MAKING THE TRAY

9 Mark the tray parts on the 9 mm MDF and check that they are square. Using a circular saw with a rip guide or a guiding batten clamped to the board, cut the 50 mm strips and the base panel a little oversize. Use a smoothing plane to bring the parts to the finished width.

10 Cut the tray parts to length on the waste side of the lines using a tenon saw. Square the ends on the smaller pieces with a block plane. The base can be left a little oversize until it is fitted.

11 Following the diagram opposite, set out the halving joints on the dividers. Cut down the sides with a tenon saw and use a 9 mm chisel to remove the waste.

12 Join the parts of the tray frame with 30 mm panel pins and adhesive.

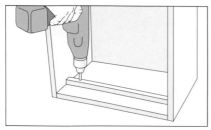

6 Mark the position of the support cleats on the chest ends and attach the cleats with screws and adhesive.

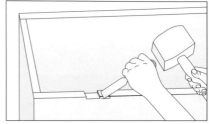

8 Cut the hinge recess on the box with a tenon saw and remove waste with a 25 mm chisel and mallet.

Make sure the joints are flush on the top and bottom and at the sides and nail a piece of timber diagonally across the frame to keep it square while the adhesive sets. Punch the heads of the panel pins below the surface. When the adhesive is dry, fit the dividers inside the tray and make adjustments if necessary. Check the dividers are square before attaching them with panel pins and adhesive.

13 Bring the tray bottom to size with a smoothing plane and check that it is square. Mark the screw holes 4.5 mm from the edges (see the diagram). Drill the 4 mm clearance holes, turn the base over and countersink the holes. Remove the brace from the frame and attach the bottom to one edge with 20 mm ($^3/_4$ in) x No. 6 gauge screws. Square the tray sides with the bottom and attach the remaining sides.

14 Place the hinge rail face up on a work surface. Cut the remaining piano hinge to length, file and open it flat. Place one leaf on the rail so the hinge knuckle is in line with the edge of the rail and centrally located in length. Drill 2 mm pilot holes in the hinge rail and attach the hinge with a few 16 mm ($^5/_8$ in) x No. 4 gauge screws. Hold the hinge rail against the tray. Place the loose leaf of the hinge on the tray so that the leaf edge is flush with the inside of the tray. Mark and drill the 2 mm holes in the edge of the tray and attach the hinge. Drill three 5 mm

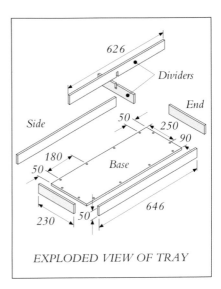

626

Dividers

End

Side

50

250

90

180

50

Base

230

50

646

EXPLODED VIEW OF TRAY

clearance holes in the face of the hinge rail (see diagram on page 39) and countersink the holes.

15 Cut two pivot bars from the scrap 9 mm MDF. Round over the ends with a block plane and sand back the rough edges. Mark the positions of the two 4 mm clearance holes 93 mm apart on each pivot bar, and centred across the width of the bar. Drill and countersink the holes (one from each side). Following the

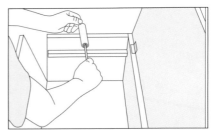

15 Drill a 2 mm pilot hole, place a washer between each pivot bar and the chest and attach the pivot bars.

The box lid opens to reveal a tray attached by a hinge and pivot bars.

diagram on page 43, mark the screw position for attaching the pivot bars to the sides of the chest. Drill 2 mm pilot holes, place washers between the pivot bars and the chest, and fasten the pivot bars using 25 mm (1 in) x No. 6 gauge countersunk screws. Tighten the screws, then loosen a little so the bars move freely.

ASSEMBLING THE CHEST

16 Position the lid on the chest so there is an equal overhang on all

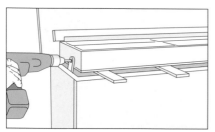

17 Sit the tray in position, using scrap material to keep it level. Attach the pivot bars to the tray sides.

sides. Copy the position of the hinges on the chest to the lid, paying careful attention when tracing around the hinge knuckles. Lay the lid on a work surface and align it with the hinging edge of the chest. Attach the hinges to the lid. Turn the chest upright and check the lid opens correctly to an angle greater than 90 degrees. Make adjustments to the lid if necessary.

17 Open the lid and lay some 9 mm scrap material across the box from front to back. Sit the tray on the scrap material. Mark the position where the hinge rail will be fixed to the lid. Drill the 3 mm pilot holes into the lid. Fold the hinge rail down and apply adhesive. Fasten the hinge rail to the lid with 32 mm (1 1/4 in) x No. 8 gauge countersunk screws.

18 Raise the pivot bars up vertically, placing washers between the tray and bars. Insert 20 mm (3/4 in) x No. 6 gauge screws and fasten the pivot bars. Remove the scrap material and test the closing of the lid. Some adjustment may be needed if the screws catch on the box sides. Countersink more screws if required.

UPHOLSTERING THE LID

19 Remove the lid from the box and sand and paint the underside before upholstering. Plane all the edges and corners of the lid so they are rounded both on top and below. Glue the foam to the top of the lid using contact adhesive.

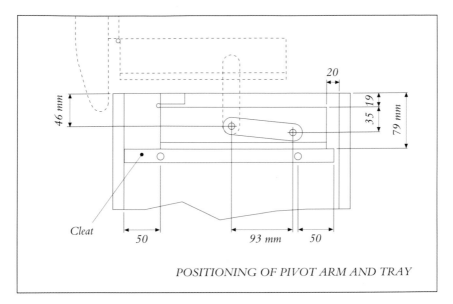

POSITIONING OF PIVOT ARM AND TRAY

20 If you have chosen a patterned fabric, centre the pattern on the lid. Put the fabric on a clean surface and place the lid on top. Pull the fabric over one long edge and attach the fabric to the centre of the edge with upholstery tacks or staples. Working outwards from the centre, continue to attach the fabric. Gently stretch the fabric towards the sides as you go and keep the pattern straight. Leave the corners open at this stage so that you can fold the corner pleats later.

Stand the lid on its edge and slide your hand across the fabric to help pull down the edges of the foam and smooth the fabric over the shoulders of the lid. Attach the fabric to the opposite edge in the same manner. Use the same technique to pull the fabric over the side edges and attach it. To fold the corner pleats, tuck one fabric edge under the other and pleat the fabric at the corner. Practise pleating the corners a few times until you have a good finish and then staple or tack the pleats into place. Remove excess fabric with scissors and use PVA adhesive to attach a piece of braiding over the edge of the fabric to hide the tacks or staples.

FINISHING THE CHEST

21 Fit all remaining screws to the hinges and fill the screw holes. Sand the chest with 180 grade abrasive paper, paying special attention to the edges. Paint the chest with a primer or sealer both inside and out. Allow to dry and sand using 240 grade abrasive paper. Apply two coats of paint, sanding gently between coats.

22 Fit a magnetic catch to the inside face of the front flap and then reassemble the box.

This blanket box was made from Australian blackwood (mahogany would be a good alternative), with stained edge beads and a clear lacquer finish. Wrought-iron handles and the tortoiseshell escutcheon plate provided finishing touches.

Blanket box

Dovetailed joints and fine timber ensure this classic blanket box will be a joy to make as well as a useful addition to the household's storage facilities. The boards in each panel are joined with dowels. This is a project for an experienced worker.

MATERIALS*

PART	MATERIAL	LENGTH	No.
Sides	150 x 25 mm timber PAR	790 mm	6
Ends	150 x 25 mm timber PAR	440 mm	6
Top	150 x 25 mm timber PAR	770 mm	3
Base	150 x 25 mm timber PAR	778 mm	3
Front trim	10 x 10 mm moulding	790 mm	2
End trim	10 x 10 mm moulding	440 mm	2

OTHER: Thirty-two 40 x 8 mm diameter timber dowels; PVA adhesive; twelve 38 mm (1 1/2 in) x No. 8 gauge countersunk wood screws; 15 mm (5/8 in) x No. 6 gauge countersunk wood screws; 30 mm panel pins; three 75 x 20 mm brass butt hinges (for cabinets); box lock (cut type with parrot-beak type catch); escutcheon plate (key hole plate); length of fine chain; two trunk handles; 25 mm wide masking tape; clear lacquer, black stain

* Finished dimensions: length 790 mm; width 440 mm, height 420 mm.

MAKING THE PANELS

1 Cut the timber roughly to length: the sides, ends, top and base are each composed of three boards. Lay the boards on a work surface and select the face sides. Match the boards as best you can for colour and grain pattern. Once the boards are matched, use chalk or crayon to place an arrow-shaped mark over the face of the boards and label each panel. Do not use pencil as it is harder to remove. Stain the trim moulding at this stage.

2 Using a jack plane, plane the meeting edges of the boards so they are straight. Use a combination

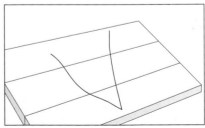

1 Match the boards for each panel and place an arrow-shaped mark over the face of the boards and label each.

TOOLS

- Chalk or crayon
- Tape measure
- Jack and smoothing planes
- Combination square and builder's roofing square
- Vice
- Marking gauge
- Dowelling jig
- Electric drill
- Utility knife

- Drill bits: 3 mm, 5 mm, 8 mm, 10 mm
- Hammer or wooden mallet
- Six 1200 mm sash cramps
- Two G-cramps
- Panel saw or circular saw
- Tenon saw or dovetail saw
- Jigsaw or coping saw

- Straight-edge
- Sliding bevel
- Bevelled-edge chisels: 25 mm and 12 mm
- Electric router (optional)
- Router bits: 12 mm straight cutting bit (for rebates); 6 mm round-over bit
- Cork sanding block or orbital sander
- Mitre box or mitre saw

square to check that the edges are square. Also check the quality of the joints by laying the boards flat and pushing the edges together, all the time looking for gaps. If necessary, adjust the edges.

3 Take the top and centre boards from one panel. Place them back to back in a vice, with their joining edges and ends flush. Find the centre of the edges and, using a square and pencil, square a line across both edges. Mark out dowel centres at

150 mm each side of the centre mark. The end panels will need three dowels and the sides, top and bottom five. Set up a marking gauge to the centre of the boards' thickness and draw a line for the dowel centres.

4 Replace the top board with the bottom board of the panel, flush the joining edges of the centre board and bottom board and mark the dowel centres as described above. Repeat this process until all the dowel centres have been marked out.

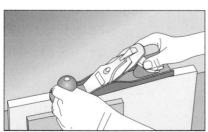

2 Use the jack plane to make the edges of the boards straight and square and remove any marks.

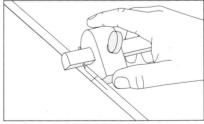

3 Mark the positions of the dowel holes along the edges and use a marking gauge to centre them.

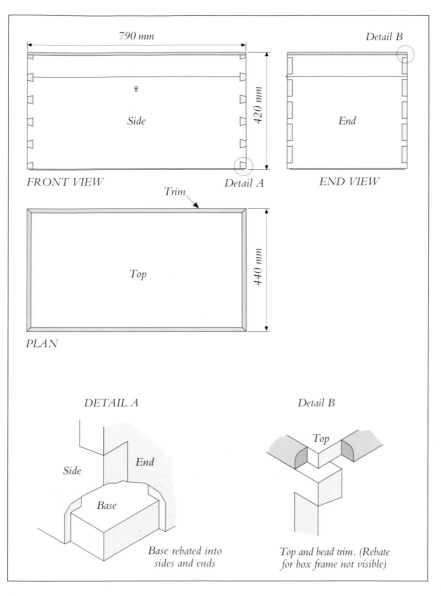

790 mm

Detail B

Side

420 mm

End

FRONT VIEW   Detail A   END VIEW

Trim

Top

440 mm

PLAN

DETAIL A   Detail B

Side   End   Top

Base

Base rebated into   Top and bead trim. (Rebate
sides and ends   for box frame not visible)

5 Set up each board in the vice and use a dowelling jig and 8 mm dowelling bit to drill each dowel hole to a depth of 21 mm. Clean around each hole to remove any torn grain, which can hold the panels apart slightly and reduce the strength of the joint. Place a small amount of adhesive into each hole and use a pencil to spread it around the

perimeter. This will also help to get rid of any excess adhesive. Place a bead of adhesive along the joining edges of the board and spread it to ensure maximum coverage. Insert the dowels in the holes and hammer them in just enough so that a little adhesive comes out from around the dowel. Bring the two boards together, tapping them with a mallet or hammer and block to protect the edges of the timber from damage. Turn the boards over and repeat the process to attach the third board.

6 Place the panel into the sash cramps with the face side up and tighten the screws to bring the joint completely together. Wipe off any excess adhesive with a clean rag. It should be possible to fit two panels into each pair of sash cramps. If the panels begin to buckle under the pressure of cramping, reduce the pressure slightly and place some weights on top of the panels, or alternatively place a third sash cramp across the top of the panel to keep it level. Leave the panels in the cramps overnight to dry.

7 Bring the side and end panels to the correct sizes. Plane one edge of the panel straight and square. From this straight-edge, mark out carefully the width and length of the panel using the roofing square to form the ends and a straight-edge for the other long edge of the panels. Score the pencil lines across the end grain of the faces and edges with a utility knife to prevent any grain breakout when you are cutting the material. Plane from each edge towards the centre to avoid chipping the edges. Use a circular saw and a straight batten held with cramps to bring the panels close to their finished sizes. Place each pair of panels in the vice together and plane the edges flush. Make sure the panels are square.

JOINING SIDES AND ENDS

8 Now set out the dovetails (see pages 54–55). Use a sharp pencil and do not cut anything until you are completely sure that the set out is correct. Don't forget to mark the waste areas clearly and check by holding the parts together that all the marked waste areas on one piece will

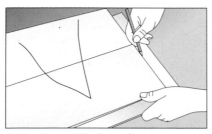

7 Use the builder's roofing square and a straight edge for squaring up the wooden panels.

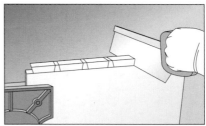

9 Cut down the sides of the tail sockets, being careful to keep to the waste side of the line.

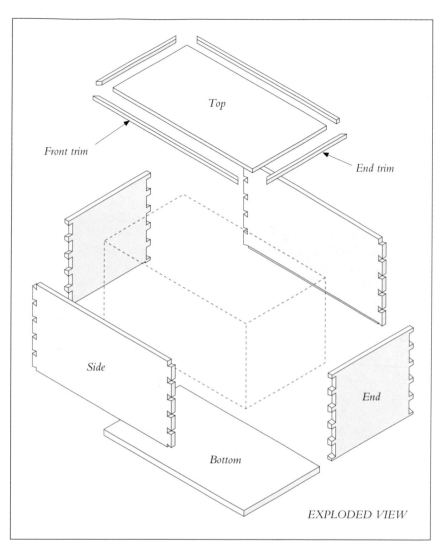

Top

Front trim

End trim

Side

End

Bottom

EXPLODED VIEW

be filled by corresponding solid areas on the joining piece. Score along the cross grain lines with a utility knife to prevent chipping out.

9 Use a tenon saw or dovetail saw to cut down the sides of the tail sockets. Keep to the waste side of the line.

Next use a jigsaw or coping saw to remove the bulk of the waste from the tail sockets. Cramp the material to a work surface making sure the tail sockets are supported by the bench. Place the cutting edge of the 25 mm bevelled-edge chisel neatly in the line made by the utility knife.

Angle the chisel slightly so you undercut the joint and, with the aid of a hammer or mallet, chisel down to about half the thickness of the timber. Chisel out all the tail sockets on the same side, and then turn the panel over and repeat the cut from the opposite side. Use the 25 mm chisel to pare down the sides of the tail sockets to remove most of the saw cut marks.

10 Take one side panel and lay it on a flat surface. Stand one end panel on the side panel as if you were joining them together. Align the joints and trace around the tail sockets with a sharp pencil to give you the exact shape for the pin sockets, as they may be slightly different from what you marked out originally. Do this for all the dovetail joints. Place the side panel in the vice and cut down the sides of the pin sockets as for the tail sockets with the tenon saw or dovetail saw, keeping to the waste side of the line and following the lines you have just made. Do not go past the knife marks.

11 Remove the waste from the pin sockets with a jigsaw or coping saw, taking care not to go past the knife lines. Lay the end panel down on the work surface as you did the side panel and chisel out the waste. Test the fitting of the joints. Make any adjustments necessary. Only a highly skilled joiner will get the joints to fit perfectly without the need for some adjustment. Tap the joints gently

together using a hammer or mallet and a block of wood to protect the faces of the timber from damage. If the half pin joints are too tight the timber may split along the grain, so take great care.

12 Take the components apart and apply adhesive to the internal faces of the joints. Bring the joints together again with the mallet and block of wood. Once all the joints are together, apply a light pressure with the sash cramps to bring them fully together. Use timber blocks to protect the face of the timber but keep the blocks back from the joints so they pull up tight. Wipe off excess adhesive with a wet rag. Check the box frame is square by measuring the diagonals. Stand the box frame to one side and allow the adhesive to dry for twenty-four hours.

ADDING TOP AND BOTTOM
13 While the box frame is drying, prepare the top panel following the method described in step 7, bringing it to a length of 780 mm in length, which is 10 mm longer than its

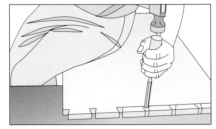

11 Cut down the sides of the pin sockets with a coping saw and then remove the waste with a chisel.

finished size. Measure the inside dimensions of the box frame and transfer them to the underside of the top, where there will be a rebate to allow the top to sit over the frame.

14 Cramp the top face down to a suitable work surface. Using a router and 12 mm rebating bit, cut a rebate in the underside of the top 9 mm deep and back to the inside dimension lines marked out in step 13. Cut across the end grain first.

15 Bring the bottom to its exact size as described in step 7. On the underside, drill four 5 mm screw holes 9 mm from each side edge, and two 5 mm screw holes 9 mm from each end edge. Countersink the holes. When the bottom is fixed it should sit 2 mm below the bottom edges of the box to protect the side timbers from breakout when the box is being moved (see Detail A in the diagram on page 47).

16 Cut a rebate in the bottom of the box frame for the bottom of the box. If using a router, make two or three

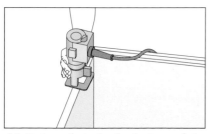

16 Cut a rebate in the bottom of the box frame. If using a router you will need two or three passes.

CUTTING REBATES WITH A ROUTER

When using a router with a straight cutting bit to make the rebates, use a backing piece to prevent chipping out the top and bottom edges when the bit comes through. For the best results, don't cut the full depth of the rebate the first time. Take off half the amount required in the first pass, adjust the router and finish the rebate to the correct depth in the second pass.

---

passes as the amount of material to be removed is quite large. Set the cutter depth to 19 mm and, if you have one, a following wheel width of cut to 4 mm (gradually increase this width until you have a rebate width of 15 mm). The following wheel will run around the inside perimeter of the box. If you don't have a following wheel, run a fence along the outer perimeter of the box but the direction of feed for the router will have to be reversed and it will have to be lowered carefully over the edge of the box to avoid mishaps. You must be very careful to ensure the cutter stops near the end of the box and does not pass through the end of it. With the rebates cut, square out the rounded corners using a 25 mm chisel and mallet.

17 Check that the top and bottom edges of the frame sides are flush at the joints. If they are not flush use a

smoothing plane to flush them off. Use a good bead of adhesive in the rebate for the bottom panel. Place the bottom in the rebate, insert the 38 mm (1¹/₂ in) x No. 8 gauge screws and drive them into position just below the surface. Use a wet rag to clean off any excess adhesive.

18 Place a bead of adhesive in the rebate of the top and spread it evenly across both faces of the joint. With a damp cloth, clean off any excess adhesive running down the inside face of the box. Lay the top in position and hold it down with sash cramps. While it is in the cramps, insert 30 mm panel pins through the sides and into the top to secure the joint. The pins should be located 8 mm down from the top edge and angled slightly to go into the top. Leave to dry.

MAKING THE LID

19 Use a combination square to mark the line where the lid will be cut off. Draw the line around the entire outside of the box. The saw cut should pass through the centre of the first dovetail pin (see the diagram on page 47). Use a circular saw with a narrow blade to make the cut and use a clamped batten or a rip guide attached to the saw to guide the saw along the cutting line.

20 Plane the closing edges of the lid and the box so that they are smooth and even, and check that they fit neatly together. Take a brass butt hinge, hold it on the back edge of the box flush with one end and mark the position one hinge length in from the end. Move the hinge to this mark and mark off the length of the hinge. Do this at both ends of the hinging edge—the centre hinge should be evenly spaced between the two outer hinges.

Hold the lid up against the box in the open position and transfer the hinge marks to the lid. Square the lines across the edge using a combination square. Set the combination square to half the width of the open hinge and mark off the width of the hinge mortise. Use a utility knife to cut across the end grain of the hinge mortise, and then

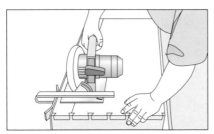

19 Use a circular saw with a narrow blade to cut off the lid. Here, a rip guide is used to guide the saw.

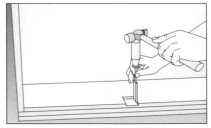

22 Lay the box with the front face down on a work surface and mark out the mortise for the lock.

use a chisel or router to remove the waste to a depth equal to the thickness of the hinge leaf. Use the screws provided or 15 mm (⁵/₈ in) x No. 6 gauge countersunk wood screws to fix the hinges into position.

FINISHING

21 To fit the lock, mark a centre line on the top edge at the front of the box and transfer the line using a square and pencil across the edge and down the inner and outer faces. Measure the position of the keyhole and transfer these measurements to the centre line on the face. Double check the position of the keyhole, and select an appropriate size of drill bit to drill the keyhole. The size of the bit will be determined by the type of keyhole plate (escutcheon).

22 Lay the box with the front face down on a work surface and continue to mark out the mortise for the lock. It is best to hold the lock flush to the top edge and trace around the perimeter of the lock with a sharp pencil and across the grain with a utility knife.

23 Fit the lid to the box and make any adjustments necessary to ensure a good fit. Mark the position of the striker plate of the lock on the lid and attach it. Now fit the escutcheon plate to the front of the box.

24 Fit a piece of fine chain to the inside of the lid to run between lid and the main frame. This will prevent the lid from opening back too far and bursting the hinges and dovetail joints.

25 Cut a rebate around the edge of the top of the lid. If using a router, set the fence at 9 mm width of cut and the cutter to 9 mm depth. Cut across the ends first and then along the sides. Hold the 10 x 10 mm moulding in the rebate and mark the inside corners of the rebates. Use a utility knife to mark the mitres on the trim pieces and cut the mitres with a tenon saw and mitre box or mitre saw if you have one.

26 Run a bead of adhesive along the rebate, place the trim in position and fasten it with masking tape. When the adhesive has set, plane the excess trim flush with the sides and top of the lid. Place a 6 mm round-over bit in the router and round over the top edges of the lid.

27 Fit the handles to the two ends of the box, placing them in the centre and a little towards the top. Then remove the handles, lock and hinge, and use an orbital sander with 120 grade abrasive paper to sand the entire box inside and out. Clean out the sanding dust from the box using a vacuum cleaner or by sweeping the surfaces with a dustpan and brush.

28 Finish the box with clear lacquer, or as desired, and make sure you seal the inside faces as well. Refit the hardware to the box.

MAKING DOVETAIL JOINTS

1 Decide which component will have the tails and which the pins. Mark them clearly.

2 There is no hard-and-fast rule about the sizes of pins and tails used for dovetail joints—it all depends on the required strength and the appearance you want. For the main project described earlier, we have used narrow pins and very wide tails for optimum appearance; the example below uses tails roughly 1¹/₂ times as thick as the pins for optimum strength. What is important is that the pins are all equal in size and that the tails are all the same size—so a bit of mathematics is required. Half-pins (angled on one side) can either be the same thickness as full pins (as shown below) or half the thickness.

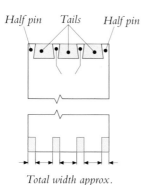

Half pin   Tails   Half pin

*Total width approx.
1¹/₂ times pin width*

3 Take the component that is to have the pins, and set out half pins (here full width) at either end. Using a combination square and pencil, mark a centre line down each half pin.

Pin lines

Centre lines

4 Take a rule and set it diagonally across the component. Move it until it is positioned with one number on each of the half pin centre lines. Divide the distance by the number of tails required (in this example, 3).

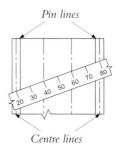

Pin lines

Centre lines

5 Mark these points: they will be the centre line positions for the full pins. Use a square to transfer them to the end of the component, measure half the pin width on either side and square the lines down the face.

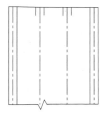

6 Set up a pitch angle (1:6 for softwoods, 1:8 for hardwoods).

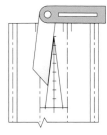

7 Set up a sliding bevel to this pitch angle and mark the angles for the pins across the end grain.

8 Mark the thickness of the joining timber across the end of each piece where the joint is to be formed.

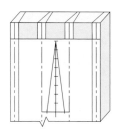

9 Use a combination square to carry the pin lines down the two faces to the marked line on both

sides. Mark out the tail sockets as waste. Use a utility knife to cut the fibres across at the tail sockets only. Cut out the tail sockets (as explained on page 49).

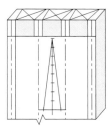

10 Stand the pin piece on its end on top of the tail piece flush with the end as shown below. With a sharp pencil, trace around the pins. Now transfer the marks to the opposite side of the tail piece. Mark the pin socket waste and use a utility knife to cut across the grain of the pin socket on both sides and edges of the material and cut out the pin sockets in

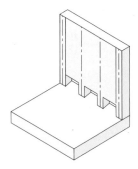

the same way. Clean up all the pins and sockets with a bevelled-edge chisel.

Whether made to fit a bay window or used as a bench box to sit below a conventional window, this seat will be a practical addition to your home. The decorative moulding can be painted to contrast.

Window seat with moulded front

This window seat with decorative moulding has been made to fit into a bay window, but you can alter it to suit your window dimensions and shape. It has a large capacity for storage, with a hinged lid for convenient access.

TOOLS

- Carpenter's square and pencil
- Circular saw
- Electric drill
- Tenon saw
- Screwdriver (cross-head or slotted)
- Folding rule or tape measure
- Combination square
- Two quick-release clamps
- Filling knife and nail punch
- Hammer
- Jack plane and smoothing plane
- Sliding bevel
- Utility knife
- Mitre saw or mitre box
- Saw horses or portable workbench
- Orbital electric sander (optional)
- Drill bits: 5 mm, 3 mm, 2 mm, countersink

CUTTING THE PIECES

1 Measure your window and adjust the measurements and side angles to suit. Lay the MDF on saw horses. Mark out the main parts using the rule, carpenter's square and pencil. Draw the longest pieces near the edges so they can be cut first. Mark all edges to be angled with a cross.

Make sure the parts are square. Leave 5 mm between them for saw cuts.

2 Cramp a batten to the board to guide the circular saw and cut the parts to width. Don't cut to length.

3 Set up a sliding bevel to the angle of the bay and mark the angled ends on the base. Cut with a circular saw. Measure the width of the angled ends and make sure that they match the width of the sides.

4 On the 490 mm wide board, square a line across one end and cut a mitre. Mark the width of a side and cut the panel. Repeat for the other side. On each side panel, draw a line 37 mm from the bottom edge and mark the screw holes, 80 mm from each end and one in the centre. Drill and countersink the 5 mm holes. Attach the sides to the base using 40 mm chipboard screws and adhesive so that the sides overlap the base by 25 mm. Plane the sides flush with the base at the front and back.

5 Place the box frame face down and check the length of the back. Mark the length on the back panel,

MATERIALS*

PART	MATERIAL	LENGTH	WIDTH	NO.
Top (left, right)	15 mm MDF	435 mm	405 mm	2
Lid	15 mm MDF	1327 mm	405 mm	1
Front	15 mm MDF	2104 mm	490 mm	1
Sides	15 mm MDF	566 mm	490 mm	2
Back	15 mm MDF	1324 mm	490 mm	1
Base	15 mm MDF	2028 mm	355 mm	1
Front skirting	15 mm MDF	2176 mm	90 mm	1
Side skirting	15 mm MDF	609 mm	90 mm	2
Front glue block	15 mm MDF	445 mm	40 mm	2
Rear glue block	15 mm MDF	445 mm	60 mm	2
Stiffening rail	15 mm MDF	1269 mm	70 mm	1
Front frame (centre)	25 mm moulding	984 mm	45 mm	2
Front frame (verticals)	25 mm moulding	279 mm	45 mm	6
Front frame (sides)	25 mm moulding	380 mm	45 mm	4
Front panel (centre)	15 mm MDF	744 mm	70 mm	1
Front panels (sides)	15 mm MDF	130 mm	70 mm	2
Cleat (rear)	15 mm MDF	1200 mm	29 mm	1
Cleats (front)	15 mm MDF	900 mm	29 mm	2

OTHER: Three 75 mm butt hinges (semi-recessed); forty-five 25 mm (1 in) x No. 6 gauge countersunk screws (cross-head or slotted); six 15 mm (5/8 in) x No. 6 gauge countersunk screws (cross-head or slotted); thirty-four 40 mm chipboard screws; sixteen 40 mm nails; panel pins: twenty-eight 30 mm and six 25 mm; PVA adhesive; abrasive paper: two sheets of 180 grade and one sheet each of 120 and 240 grade; primer/sealer; paint; wood filler

* Finished dimensions: length 2200 mm; width 420 mm; height 505 mm. Don't pre-cut the components to their exact lengths until you need them.

including the mitres, and cut the panel a millimetre over size with the circular saw blade set at the appropriate angle for the mitre. Draw lines 11 mm in from either end on the back face and mark three screw holes 60 mm from the top and the bottom, and one in the centre. Carefully drill 5 mm holes at an angle of 45 degrees and countersink.

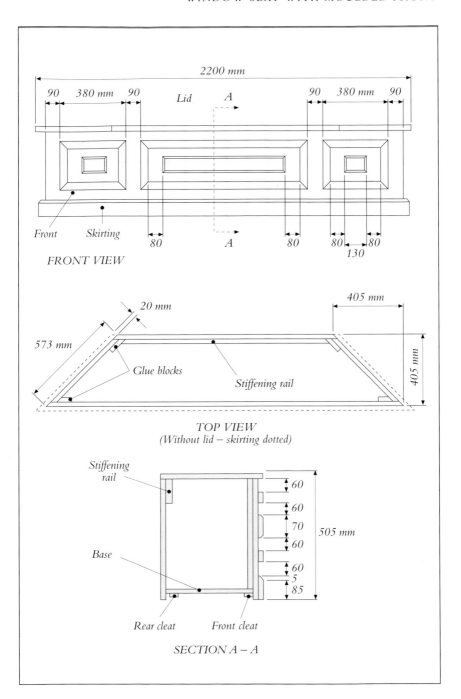

FRONT VIEW

TOP VIEW
(Without lid – skirting dotted)

SECTION A – A

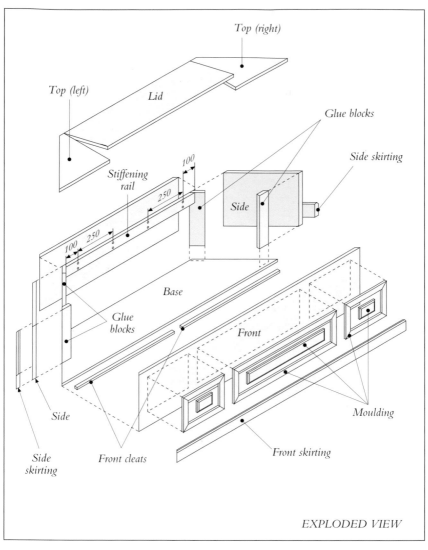

Top (right)

Top (left)

Lid

Glue blocks

Side skirting

Stiffening rail

100

250

250

100

Side

Base

Glue blocks

Front

Side

Side skirting

Front cleats

Front skirting

Moulding

EXPLODED VIEW

6 Draw a line 37 mm from the bottom edge along the back panel and mark the five screw holes, 100 mm and 250 mm from each end, and one in the centre. Drill and countersink 5 mm clearance holes. Apply adhesive to the edges, position

the back on the box frame and attach using 40 mm chipboard screws. Cut and attach the front panel in a similar manner. Plane all the joints flush.

7 Cut four glue blocks and angle one long edge of each. Plane the angled

edge and glue the blocks in place in each corner.

8 Cut the stiffening rail and angle one end. Hold the rail in place and mark off the length. Cut the other angle. Attach with eight 25 mm (1 in) x No. 6 gauge screws and PVA adhesive and cramp in place.

9 Turn the box on its back. Cut the three cleats, clamp them in place and attach them with adhesive and three 25 mm (1 in) x No. 6 gauge screws in each front cleat and four screws in the rear one. Turn the box upright. Insert two screws through the bottom into each front cleat, and three screws into the rear cleat.

FITTING THE LID

10 Mark and cut out the top panels so they overhang 20 mm at the sides and front. Draw a line 28 mm in from the side and front edges of each top. Attach the tops to the sides and front with 40 mm nails and adhesive.

11 Position two hinges 75 mm from either end of the lid, and the third in

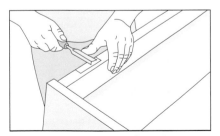

11 Mark the position of the hinges on the top edge of the back and remove the waste with a 25 mm chisel.

The decorative moulding can be painted to contrast with the box.

the middle. Mark the hinge position on the top edge of the back and square the lines over the edge. Mark the width of the leaf on the back and remove the waste with a 25 mm chisel. Position the hinges, drill 2 mm pilot holes, and attach with 25 mm (1 in) x No. 6 gauge screws. Place the box on its back propped up on 15 mm MDF off-cuts and align the lid. Drill 2 mm pilot holes in the lid and attach the lid with one screw per hinge. Stand the box upright and check the fit before using the remaining screws.

FINISHING THE BOX

12 From the MDF offcuts, cut the side skirting over length. Cut a mitre at one end, hold the skirting in place, and mark and cut the other mitre. Attach the side skirting using PVA adhesive and three 25 mm (1 in) x No. 6 gauge screws from the inside of the box, making sure the front of

mitre is flush with the front of the box and the screws are countersunk. (Only attach the skirting temporarily if you plan to bevel the edges.) Mark and cut the front skirting and attach it from the inside of the box using five screws evenly spaced. If required, remove the skirting and bevel or round over the top edge and corners. Sand with 120 grade abrasive paper.

13 Lay the box on its back and mark out the size and position of the mouldings. Cut out the vertical frame parts (a mitre box or mitre saw will help) and attach to the box with 30 mm panel pins and PVA adhesive. Make sure all parts are parallel to each other. From the vertical parts, mark the length of the horizontal pieces. Cut the mitres and attach the horizontal frame parts. Cut the centre panels from 15 mm MDF and attach them using the 25 mm panel pins and adhesive.

14 Punch the nail heads below the surface of the box and fill the holes. Use 120 grade abrasive paper to sand

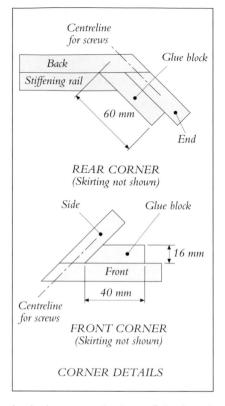

REAR CORNER
(Skirting not shown)

Centreline for screws
Back
Stiffening rail
Glue block
60 mm
End

Side
Glue block
16 mm
Front
40 mm
Centreline for screws

FRONT CORNER
(Skirting not shown)

CORNER DETAILS

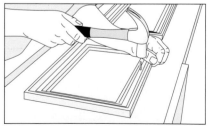

13 Attach the front mouldings with panel pins and adhesive and punch the nail heads below the surface.

back the exposed edges of the board to a smooth finish. Don't sand the surface of the MDF as it tends to 'fur up' after the paint has been applied if sanded too heavily. Apply one coat of primer or sealer, paying particular attention to the edges. When the sealer is dry, use 180 grade abrasive paper to sand to a smooth finish.

15 Apply the first coat of paint, allow to dry and sand back with 240 grade abrasive paper. Then apply the second coat. If you need to, sand the box again with 240 grade abrasive before applying a third coat of paint.

Tools for making boxes

Some of the most useful tools for making boxes are shown below. Build up your tool kit gradually—most of the tools can be purchased from your local hardware store.

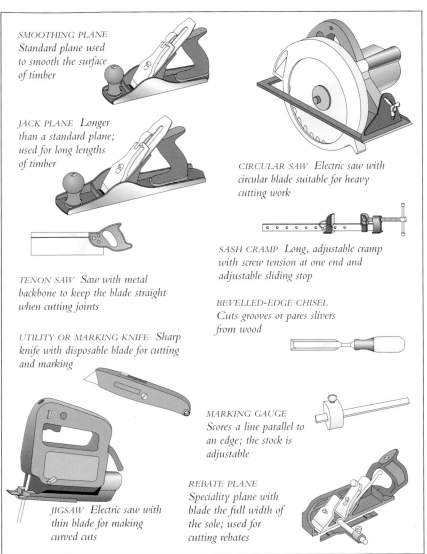

SMOOTHING PLANE
Standard plane used
to smooth the surface
of timber

JACK PLANE Longer
than a standard plane;
used for long lengths
of timber

CIRCULAR SAW Electric saw with
circular blade suitable for heavy
cutting work

SASH CRAMP Long, adjustable cramp
with screw tension at one end and
adjustable sliding stop

TENON SAW Saw with metal
backbone to keep the blade straight
when cutting joints

BEVELLED-EDGE CHISEL
Cuts grooves or pares slivers
from wood

UTILITY OR MARKING KNIFE Sharp
knife with disposable blade for cutting
and marking

MARKING GAUGE
Scores a line parallel to
an edge; the stock is
adjustable

REBATE PLANE
Speciality plane with
blade the full width of
the sole; used for
cutting rebates

JIGSAW Electric saw with
thin blade for making
curved cuts

Index

Stencil

Rocking horse stencil (page 25)